INFORMATION EXPLORER JUNIOR

Take Note! Taking and Organizing Notes

by Ellen Range

CHERRY LAKE PUBLISHING · ANN ARBOR, MICHIGAN

A NOTE TO PARENTS AND TEACHERS: Please remind your children how to stay safe online before they do the activities in this book.

A NOTE TO KIDS: Always remember your safety comes first!

Published in the United States of America
by Cherry Lake Publishing
Ann Arbor, Michigan
www.cherrylakepublishing.com

Content Adviser: Gail Dickinson, PhD, Associate Professor, Old Dominion University, Norfolk, Virginia

Photo Credits: Cover, ©Kzenon/Shutterstock.com; page 5, ©Syda Productions/Shutterstock.com; page 6, ©Zurijeta/Shutterstock.com; pages 9 and 14, ©Monkey Business Images/Shutterstock.com.

Library of Congress Cataloging-in-Publication Data
Range, Ellen.
   Take note! : Taking and organizing notes / By Ellen Range.
      pages cm. — (Information Explorer Junior)
   Includes bibliographical references and index.
   Audience: K to Grade 3.
   ISBN 978-1-63137-788-4 (lib. bdg.) — ISBN 978-1-63137-848-5 (e-book) — ISBN 978-1-63137-808-9 (pbk.) — ISBN 978-1-63137-828-7 (pdf)
   1. Note-taking—Juvenile literature. I. Title. II. Title: Taking and organizing notes.

   LB2395.25.R36 2014
   371.3—dc23   2014001366

Cherry Lake Publishing would like to acknowledge the work of The Partnership for 21st Century Skills. Please visit *www.p21.org* for more information.

Printed in the United States of America
Corporate Graphics Inc.
July 2014

Table of Contents

4 CHAPTER ONE
What Is Note Taking?

8 CHAPTER TWO
Sticky Notes

12 CHAPTER THREE
Tables

16 CHAPTER FOUR
Visual Note Taking

22 Glossary
23 Find Out More
24 Index
24 About the Author

CHAPTER ONE

What Is Note Taking?

Have you ever forgotten something important? Maybe you forgot to bring your sneakers to school on gym day. Or perhaps you forgot when your friend's birthday party was supposed to start. Taking notes is one way to avoid forgetting things. Notes are short messages. You don't need to write whole sentences in notes. You just need to write the important parts. For example, a note probably wouldn't say, "Tomorrow is gym day. Don't forget to bring your sneakers!" It would say "sneakers tomorrow" or even just "sneakers."

sneakers tomorrow

You can also use notes to remember information that you read about. Sometimes your reading leads you to ideas you want to think about later. You may also make **predictions** about what will happen next. However, you might forget about these ideas as you keep reading. Taking notes as you read is a great way to remember your thoughts. You can look over your notes later and remember what you were thinking about as you read.

Sometimes a note can be a sketch instead of words.

Taking notes is a little like making a sandwich. You have to gather the bread and ingredients first. Then you arrange them in the right order to make a tasty snack. When taking notes, you have to gather the information first. Then you put it together in a way that makes sense to you. There are many ways to take notes. In this book, we'll look at some note-taking **strategies**.

Just like when making a sandwich, notes should be organized in a logical order.

To get a copy of this activity, visit www.cherrylakepublishing.com/activities.

Try This

Notes should use as few words as possible. For example, if a book says, "Most mice eat seeds or grass," you might make a note that reads, "Food = seeds, grass." Writing just the important words on your note saves you time! Try turning the following sentences into short notes.

1. The United States of America is made up of 50 individual states.

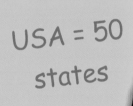

2. The basketball game will begin at 7:00 p.m.

3. The first working airplane was built and tested by brothers Orville and Wilbur Wright in 1903.

CHAPTER TWO

Sticky Notes

Using sticky notes is one popular tool to keep track of information. As you read, you may find words that seem important. You might read things that you want to remember later. You might even have questions about something in the book. Sticky notes give you a place to write down those ideas or questions. You can stick them on the side of the page you are reading. You can also keep them in a folder. As you keep reading, you may find that the book answers a question you had earlier. You can go back to your sticky notes and write down answers as you find them.

noun: person, place, thing

conjunction: connecting word

What should you write down? Think about the main idea of the book and other information that seems important. Then ask yourself two questions: (1) What did I learn from what I read? and (2) What do I need to remember? Take notes when you find information that could answer these questions. Use a new sticky note for each new idea.

circle = Πr^2

$E = mc^2$

Write notes as you read. You may forget things if you wait until later.

Sticky notes come in many colors. Ella likes to use different colors for different kinds of notes. This helps her organize her information. She uses green notes for information about important people. Pink notes are used for dates. Blue notes mark new **vocabulary** words. When she looks at her notes later, the colors make it easy to find different kinds of information.

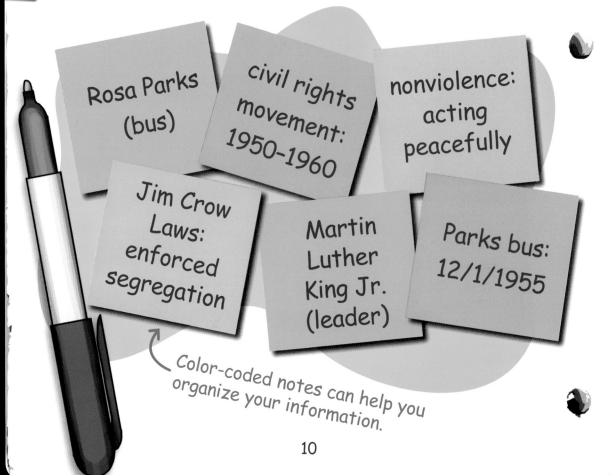

Rosa Parks (bus)

civil rights movement: 1950–1960

nonviolence: acting peacefully

Jim Crow Laws: enforced segregation

Martin Luther King Jr. (leader)

Parks bus: 12/1/1955

Color-coded notes can help you organize your information.

Try This

Visit the library and check out a book about an animal. Then grab a pencil and some sticky notes. Read your book and look closely for interesting facts. Write each piece of information down on a new sticky note. Stick each note along the edge of the page where you found the information. You can also write down questions you have as you read. For example, a book about cats might make you wonder, "How do cats always land on their feet?"

Look over your notes once you have finished the book. Did your questions get answered? How did your notes help you keep track of useful information?

CHAPTER THREE

Tables

MY NOTE TABLE

Creating a table is another good strategy for note taking. Tables organize your information into **columns** and **rows**. They can make it easier to see what information you have found and what you still need to learn.

Mia's teacher has asked her to research a famous person, Rosa Parks. Mia needs to find out when Parks was born, where she lived, and what made her famous. A table is a great way to organize this information.

To make a table, Mia draws a box on a piece of paper. Then she draws some lines across to make rows. She draws lines up and down to make columns. Next, she labels the top of the table "Rosa Parks." In the first column, Mia writes the questions that her teacher assigned. She puts one question in each box of the column. Now she knows what to look for as she researches. Next to each question, Mia has a box for writing the answer!

Rosa Parks

When was she born?	
Where did she live?	
What made her famous?	

A table helps you keep track of what information to look for.

Mia writes down only the most useful information she finds. If she tried to write down everything, it would be harder to find what she is looking for later. Her hand would get tired, too!

Try This

An interview gives you a chance to learn about people's experiences.

Not all information comes from books. You can learn a lot just by talking to people! An interview is a time for you to ask someone questions. Try using a table to organize information for an interview.

To get a copy of this activity, visit www.cherrylakepublishing.com/activities.

1. Find someone who is willing to talk with you. This could be a family member or a friend.

2. In one column of your table, write down five things you want to know about that person. Maybe you want to ask about the person's favorite food or hobbies.

3. Ask the person each question.

4. Write down the answers in the second column of your table. Remember to keep your notes short and simple.

5. When you are done asking questions, thank the person for letting you conduct the interview.

Thank you for taking the time to answer my questions.

CHAPTER FOUR

Visual Note Taking

We have learned that there are many ways to take notes. You can mark important ideas or keep track of questions with sticky notes. You can also use tables to arrange your notes. Making sketches or drawings is another way to get ideas on paper. You can draw pictures to add to your writing, make a map, or create a flowchart. Flowcharts use arrows, words, and images to show the steps of a process. Imagine that your teacher has explained how tadpoles grow into frogs.

Flowcharts can show a life cycle or other process.

A flowchart with pictures and arrows can help you see this process more clearly.

Jeremy and his family are taking a trip to the state of Michigan. They want to visit some state parks along their route. Jeremy labels all the parks they will be driving by on a map of Michigan. The labeled map shows them how many parks there are. It also shows how far apart the parks are.

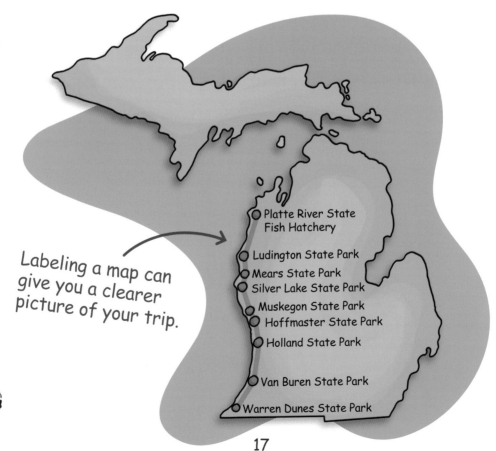

Labeling a map can give you a clearer picture of your trip.

Platte River State Fish Hatchery

Ludington State Park
Mears State Park
Silver Lake State Park
Muskegon State Park
Hoffmaster State Park
Holland State Park

Van Buren State Park

Warren Dunes State Park

Sometimes you might want to compare two or more things. Try using a **Venn diagram** to organize this information. A Venn diagram is a drawing of circles that **overlap**. On a sheet of unlined paper, draw two circles. Label each circle with the name of one of the things you are comparing. Put things that are only true for one topic in the big part of the circle. In the overlapping part, write down things that the topics have in common. Annie wants to learn about the planet Venus. She is curious how

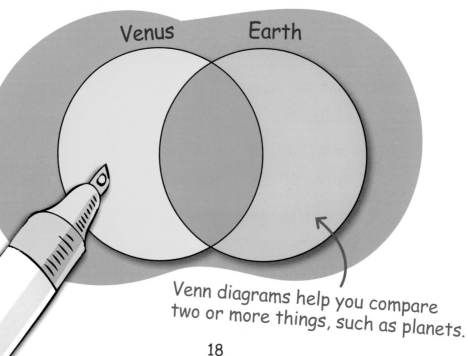

Venn diagrams help you compare two or more things, such as planets.

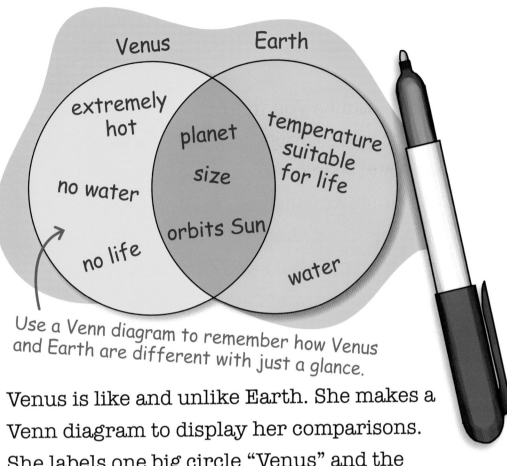

Venus

Earth

extremely hot

no water

no life

planet size

orbits Sun

temperature suitable for life

water

Use a Venn diagram to remember how Venus and Earth are different with just a glance.

Venus is like and unlike Earth. She makes a Venn diagram to display her comparisons. She labels one big circle "Venus" and the other "Earth." She includes weather, color, and size in her diagram. Where the circles overlap, she writes things that the planets have in common. Things they don't have in common stay in the separate bigger circles.

Another type of visual notes is the web-shaped drawing. These drawings are often called mind maps, word webs, or graphic organizers. Gabe uses a web-shaped drawing

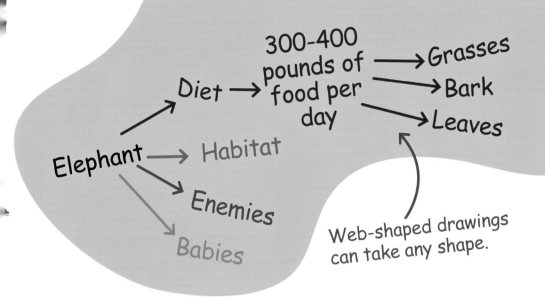

Web-shaped drawings can take any shape.

to learn about elephants. He writes his topic, elephant, in the middle. Then he draws lines outward and puts important ideas about the animal at the end of each line. He includes information about the animal's diet, habitat, enemies, and babies. As he learns more about each of these smaller topics, he draws more lines going outward.

Remember that note taking is personal. The method that works best for you may not work for your friend. Also, the same method may not work for every task. Don't be afraid to try out different note-taking strategies. You are on your way to becoming a note-taking expert!

Try This

Book #1

Book #2

Try making a Venn diagram of your own!

- Think about two of your favorite books or stories. Draw two circles that overlap.
- In one circle of your diagram, write down your favorite things about Book #1.
- In the other circle, write down your favorite things about Book #2.
- In the overlapping section, write down everything you can think of that relates to both books. Do they both have happy endings? Can you read all of the words in both books without help? Are both books about a dog?
- When you're finished, look at the information you have gathered. What has this Venn diagram taught you about your favorite books? This information could help you find new books to read!

To get a copy of this activity, visit www.cherrylakepublishing.com/activities.

Glossary

columns (KAH-luhmz) series of numbers or words that run up and down in a chart or table

overlap (oh-vur-LAP) to extend over or partly cover something

predictions (prih-DIK-shunz) things you think will happen in the future

rows (ROHZ) series of numbers or words that run side to side in a chart or table

strategies (STRAT-uh-jeez) plans for achieving a goal

Venn diagram (VEHN DYE-uh-gram) a graph that organizes information using overlapping circles

vocabulary (voh-KAB-yuh-ler-ee) all the words that a person can use and understand

Find Out More

BOOKS

Gaines, Ann Graham. *Ace Your Research Paper*. Berkeley Heights, NJ: Enslow Publishers, 2009.

Green, Julie. *Write It Down*. Ann Arbor, MI: Cherry Lake Publishing, 2010.

Rabbat, Suzy. *Citing Sources: Learning to Use the Copyright Page*. Ann Arbor, MI: Cherry Lake Publishing, 2013.

WEB SITES

Kentucky Virtual Library Presents: How to Do Research
www.kyvl.org/kids/f_homebase.html
Explore the steps of the research process, and learn how to take notes in different ways.

KidsHealth—Six Steps to Smarter Studying
http://kidshealth.org/kid/feeling/school/studying.html
Get advice for taking notes and developing good study skills.

Scholastic—Venn Diagram
http://teacher.scholastic.com/lessonplans/graphicorg/pdfs/venndiagram.pdf
Print out a blank Venn diagram.

Index

colors, 10
columns, 12, 13, 15

drawings, 16, 17

flowcharts, 16–17

ideas, 5, 8, 9, 16, 20
interviews, 14–15

length, 4, 7, 15

maps, 16, 17
mind maps, 19–20

predictions, 5

reading, 5, 8, 9, 11, 21
research, 12–13
rows, 12

sketches, 16, 17
sticky notes, 7, 8–10, 11, 16
style, 20

tables, 12–13, 14–15, 16

Venn diagrams, 18–19, 21

web-shaped drawings, 19–20
word webs, 19–20

About the Author

Ellen Range is a graduate student from southern Minnesota. She is studying school library media and library and information science at the University of Michigan.